NO FLUFF. JUST REAL STEPSIF

YOU'RE TIRED OF BEING BROKE, READ THIS

A SIMPLE, HONEST GUIDE TO ESCAPING FINANCIAL STRESS & BUILDING REAL STABILITY

MOISE GLORIANIE

This book is a work of nonfiction written for educational and informational purposes only. It is not intended as financial, legal, or professional advice. The author is not a licensed financial advisor. Readers are encouraged to use their own judgment and, where appropriate, consult qualified professionals before making financial decisions.

The experiences, explanations, and examples shared in this book are intended to help readers better understand money habits and financial stability. Individual results may vary based on personal circumstances, choices, and external factors.

First published in 2025

TABLE OF CONTENTS

INTRODUCTION

This book was not written to impress anyone.

It was written because I know what it feels like to worry about money.

I know the stress of checking your account and hoping there is enough.

I know the fear of unexpected bills.

I know the feeling of working hard and still feeling stuck.

For a long time, I thought something was wrong with me.

I thought being broke meant I failed.

But the truth is simple.

Most people were never taught how to manage money in a clear and honest way.

They were taught to survive, not to plan.

They were taught to work, not to think.

This book is not about getting rich fast.

It is about getting stable.

It is about having peace.

It is about feeling in control again.

I wrote this book in very simple language on purpose.

No big words.

No complicated ideas.

No pressure.

You don’t need to be perfect to improve your finances.

You just need clarity.

This book will help you understand:

- Why money feels so stressful
- Why working harder is not always the answer
- How small choices affect your future
- How to build stability step by step

If you feel tired of being broke, you are not weak.

You are tired because you care.

This book is for people who want real change, not fake promises.

For people who want progress, not pressure.

For people who want peace, not panic.

If you read this book slowly and apply what makes sense to you,

your relationship with money will change.

And when that changes,

everything else begins to feel lighter.

WHO THIS BOOK IS FOR

This book is for the person who feels tired deep inside.

Not just tired from work,

but tired from worrying. Tired from trying.

Tired from carrying the weight alone.

This book is for the person who works hard, does their best,

and still feels like it’s never enough. You pay your bills.

You show up. You keep going.

But somehow, peace always feels out of reach.

This book is for the person who feels anxious when money is mentioned.

The one who avoids checking their bank account.

The one who feels shame, fear, or frustration

instead of control. Not because you are careless.

Not because you are lazy.

But because no one ever taught you a simple, calm way to manage money.

This book is for the person who feels stuck in

survival mode. Living paycheck to paycheck.

Making decisions out of pressure, not clarity.

Always reacting.

Never breathing.

This book is for the person who doesn’t want quick money or empty promises.

You don’t want hype. You don’t want shortcuts.

You want stability.

You want peace.

You want to feel safe again.

This book is for the person who is ready to stop blaming themselves.

Ready to stop feeling behind.

Ready to believe that change can happen without shame or punishment.

You don’t need to be perfect.

You don’t need to have it all together.

You don’t need to change everything at once. You just need honesty.

You need clarity.

You need a place to start.

If you are ready to slow down, to understand your money,

and to build a calmer, more stable life— this book was written for you.

And you are not late. You are right on time.

PART 1

UNDERSTANDING THE PROBLEM

CHAPTER 1

BEING BROKE IS MORE THAN MONEY

Being broke is not just about having less money.

It is about how you feel every day.

It is the stress that follows you when you wake up.

It is the fear that comes when your phone rings.

It is the pressure in your mind when bills are due.

Money problems do not stay in your wallet.

They live in your thoughts.

When money is tight, your emotions change.

You feel anxious.

You feel frustrated.

You feel stuck.

That is why money controls emotions.

Not because money is powerful,

but because uncertainty is scary.

When you don’t know how things will work out,

your mind stays on alert.

You think too much.

You sleep less.

You lose peace.

I have learned that this is why people feel tired all the time.

Not because they don’t try,

but because their mind never rests.

Many people blame themselves.

They think being broke means they are bad with money.

They think they are failing.

That is not true.

Most people were never taught how to manage money calmly and clearly.

They were taught to react, not to plan.

They were taught to survive, not to build.

This book is different.

It does not judge you.

It does not rush you.

It does not promise miracles.

This book helps you understand why you feel the way you do about money.

It helps you slow down.

It helps you see clearly.

Because once you understand the problem,

you stop blaming yourself.

And when blame disappears,

change becomes possible.

CHAPTER 2

WORKING HARD IS NOT THE SAME AS MOVING FORWARD

Many people work very hard.

They wake up early.

They stay busy all day.

They feel tired at night.

Yet nothing changes.

This is confusing.

It is frustrating.

It is painful.

You start asking yourself,

"If I'm working so hard, why am I still stuck?"

The truth is simple.

Effort alone does not fix finances.

Working hard without direction is like running in place.

You use energy.

You get tired.

But you don’t move forward.

Being busy feels productive,

but being busy does not always mean progress.

This is the trap.

People stay busy to feel useful.

They take extra hours.

They say yes to everything.

They push themselves harder and harder.

But when money is not managed with intention,

more effort only creates more exhaustion.

This is how people become busy but broke.

They earn money,

but they don’t control it.

They receive income,

but they don’t see progress.

Income is what comes in.

Progress is what stays.

Many people confuse the two.

You can make more money

and still feel stressed.

You can earn more

and still live paycheck to paycheck.

That is because progress is not about how much you make.

It is about what you do with what you have.

Progress means:

- Having a simple plan
- Making intentional choices
- Reducing stress little by little

Without these,

even a higher income can disappear.

This is not a personal failure.

It is a missing lesson.

Most people were taught to work harder,

but not taught how to manage money with clarity.

This book helps you slow down and see clearly.

It helps you understand where your effort is going.

And it helps you turn effort into forward movement.

Because when effort and direction work together, change becomes possible.

CHAPTER 3

THE LIES WE WERE TAUGHT ABOUT MONEY

Many people struggle with money not because they are careless,

but because they believe things that are not true.

These beliefs often start early.

We hear them from family.

From friends.

From society.

Over time, these ideas feel normal.

But they quietly keep people stuck.

One common lie is this:

"Just work harder."

Hard work is important.

But hard work alone is not a plan.

Many people already work hard.

They work long hours.

They sacrifice their time.

Yet they still feel stressed.

This lie makes people blame themselves.

If things don’t improve, they think they are not doing enough.

So they push harder instead of thinking differently.

Another lie is this:

“Money is evil.”

This belief creates guilt.

People feel bad wanting more stability.

They feel selfish for wanting comfort or security.

So they avoid learning about money.

But money itself is not good or bad.

Money is a tool.

Avoiding money does not make you a better person.

It only keeps you unprepared.

Another lie many people believe is:

"I'll fix it later."

Later feels safe.

Later feels less stressful.

But later often never comes.

Life gets busy.

Problems grow quietly.

Stress builds over time.

Waiting makes things harder, not easier.

These beliefs may seem small,

but they shape daily choices.

They affect how people spend.

How they save.

How they plan.

Over time, these lies create habits.

And habits create results.

This is how people stay stuck without realizing why.

This book is here to challenge those beliefs.

Not with shame.

Not with pressure.

But with understanding.

Once you question the lies you were taught,

you can choose better thoughts.

And better thoughts lead to better decisions.

Change does not start with more effort.

It starts with clearer thinking.

PART 2
CHANGING THE MINDSET

CHAPTER 4

YOU DON'T NEED MORE MONEY FIRST

Many people believe one thing:

"If I had more money, my problems would be solved."

This sounds true.

But for most people, it is not.

More money does not automatically bring peace.

More money does not automatically bring control.

Many people earn more and still feel stressed.

They still worry.

They still feel behind.

That is because money is not the first problem.

Clarity is.

When you don't understand where your money goes,

more money just moves faster.

When there is no plan,

income disappears quietly.

This is why some people make a lot of money

and still live paycheck to paycheck.

They have income,

but they don’ t have control.

Control comes before growth.

Before you earn more,

you need to understand what you already have.

You need to know:

- What comes in
- What goes out
- What truly matters

This is not about perfection.

It is about awareness.

Many people avoid looking at their money.

It feels uncomfortable.

It feels stressful.

But avoiding it gives money more power.

When you face your numbers calmly,

fear starts to lose control.

Clarity brings relief.

You don’t need to change everything at once.

You don’t need to be strict.

You don’t need to punish yourself.

You need to slow down

and pay attention.

Once you gain clarity,

better decisions become easier.

Spending becomes more intentional.

Saving feels possible.

Stress starts to fade.

More money can help later.

But clarity must come first.

Because when you understand your money,

you don’t feel lost anymore.

And when you are not lost,

progress becomes real.

CHAPTER 5

SURVIVAL MODE IS DRAINING YOUR LIFE

Many people live in survival mode.

They wake up.

They work.

They pay bills.

They sleep.

And then they do it all again.

Living paycheck to paycheck feels normal for many.

But it is exhausting.

Every decision is influenced by fear.

"Do I have enough?"

"Can I pay this bill?"

"What if something goes wrong?"

Fear is powerful.

It makes people settle.

It makes them avoid opportunities.

It makes them spend money without thinking,

just to feel relief for a moment.

When you are in survival mode, your brain is always in high alert.

It focuses on urgent problems,

not important choices.

It reacts,

instead of planning.

It moves quickly,

but rarely moves forward.

This constant stress is draining.

It takes energy,

focus,

and joy.

The good news is you can slow down.

You can pause.

You can breathe.

Start by looking at your money calmly.

Not to judge yourself.

Not to panic.

Just to see clearly.

Write down what comes in.

Write down what goes out.

Notice patterns.

Next, make small changes.

Even tiny actions reduce fear.

Maybe you save just $5 this week.

Maybe you skip one unnecessary purchase.

Every small step builds control.

Every step shows that fear does not have all the power.

And when fear loses control,

your brain can think clearly again.

You can plan.

You can grow.

You can make better decisions.

Survival mode keeps you alive.

But it does not let you thrive.

Clarity and small, intentional actions

are the first steps toward freedom.

Because when you slow down and think clearly,

you start living, not just surviving.

CHAPTER 6

FINANCIAL PEACE STARTS WITH ONE DECISION

Financial peace does not come from luck.

It does not come from a raise.

It starts with one decision.

The first step is taking responsibility.

Not blaming your job.

Not blaming the economy.

Not blaming anyone else.

This is not about shame.

It is about honesty.

It is about seeing your life clearly and saying,

"I can take control."

Many people wait for permission to start.

They wait for the right circumstances.

They wait for motivation.

But waiting only delays progress.

Choosing progress means choosing action.

Even if the first steps are small.

Even if they feel uncomfortable.

Even if you make mistakes.

One clear choice can change everything.

Deciding to track your spending.

Deciding to save something each week.

Deciding to face fear instead of hiding.

It may feel simple.

But simplicity is powerful.

A single decision creates momentum.

It opens doors that fear had kept closed.

It builds confidence that grows over time.

You do not need to fix everything at once.

You do not need to have all the answers.

You only need to make the first choice.

And then the next.

Financial peace is not about money first.

It is about choices.

It is about action.

It is about taking control, one decision at a time.

Because when you start, even with one choice,

you are no longer stuck.

You are moving forward.

And forward is where progress begins.

PART 3
SIMPLE MONEY RULES

CHAPTER 7

THAT WORK

There is one rule that can change your life.

It is simple.

It is old.

It works every time.

Spend less than you earn.

That’ s it.

It sounds almost too simple.

But simplicity is the reason it is ignored.

People want complicated solutions.

They look for tricks, hacks, or quick fixes.

They believe more money or a new strategy will solve everything.

But ignoring this rule keeps people stuck.

They earn more.

They spend more.

They stay trapped in the same cycle.

The power of this rule is in its simplicity.

When you consistently spend less than you earn, you gain control.

You reduce stress.

You create space for savings, investment, and opportunity.

Applying it does not have to be painful.

You don’t need to cut everything you enjoy.

You don’t need to live in fear of spending.

Start small.

Track your money.

Notice where it goes.

Decide what really matters.

Cut only what doesn’t serve your goals.

Adjust slowly.

Avoid extreme rules that you cannot maintain.

Even small differences add up.

Saving a little here, spending less there,

makes a big impact over time.

This is not about deprivation.

It is about freedom.

Freedom comes from control.

Control comes from living below your means.

The rule is simple, but life-changing:

Spend less than you earn.

Do it consistently.

Watch how your stress fades.

Watch how your options grow.

Watch how your life begins to change.

Because once you master this rule,

money becomes a tool, not a source of fear.

CHAPTER 8
SMALL HABITS THAT QUIETLY BREAK YOU

It’ s not always big mistakes that ruin your finances.

Most of the time, it’ s the small, quiet habits.

The ones you barely notice.

The ones that sneak in and slowly take control.

Unnoticed spending is the most common trap.

A coffee on the way to work.

A few dollars here, a few dollars there.

Subscriptions you forgot about.

A “tiny treat” every week.

It seems harmless at first.

After all, what’ s a few dollars?

But these little purchases repeat.

They grow.

Over months and years, they quietly add up to thousands of dollars gone—without you realizing.

Then there’ s emotional buying.

The stress of the day hits.

You shop to feel better.

You scroll online to escape boredom.

You buy to reward yourself for surviving life’ s challenges.

It feels good… for a moment.

But then guilt and stress come back, even stronger.

And the cycle repeats.

Why do these small habits matter so much?

Because little leaks sink big ships.

One drip might seem small.

But keep dripping every day, and the boat will eventually flood.

The same is true for your money.

Tiny, repeated spending can quietly destroy your financial freedom.

Here’s the reality: most people never notice these habits.

They focus on the big purchases—cars, houses, bills.

They ignore the small habits that steal money silently.

And that’s why progress feels impossible.

The solution is surprisingly simple—but it requires honesty.

Step one: Notice the leaks.

Track every dollar.

Write it down.

See where it really goes.

Step two: Question your spending.

Ask yourself:

“Did I need this?”

“Was I buying to solve a real problem—or just a feeling?”

“Does this move me closer to my goals, or further away?”

Step three: Replace the habit, don’t just stop it.

If you shop when stressed, replace it with a walk, exercise, or a journal.

If you grab coffee every morning, try making it at home.

If you scroll online and buy impulsively, limit the apps or set a timer.

Even small changes create big results over time.

Stop the leaks.

Watch your money grow.

Watch your stress fade.

Watch your confidence increase.

The truth is simple: big progress comes from small, consistent habits.

Fix the little things first,

and the big things—your freedom, your control, your peace—will follow.

And here’ s the secret: readers who catch these habits early don’ t just save money.

They gain power.

They gain choice.

They gain life.

Because when you understand how tiny actions shape your life,

you stop being a victim of your habits

and start being the master of your future.

CHAPTER 9
SIMPLE HABITS THAT BUILD STABILITY

Stability does not happen overnight.

It does not come from a big paycheck or a lucky break.

It comes from simple habits—small, repeated actions that build a strong foundation over time.

The key is one habit at a time.

Trying to change everything at once is overwhelming.

It leads to stress, mistakes, and giving up.

But focusing on one habit?

That is powerful.

Start small.

Maybe it's tracking every expense for a week.

Maybe it's saving $10 every week.

Maybe it's setting aside one evening to plan your budget.

One habit, consistently applied, creates momentum.

It becomes automatic.

And it leads to another habit.

Easy systems make habits stick.

Systems remove guesswork.

They turn decisions into routines.

For example:

- Automate savings so it happens before you even see the money.
- Set reminders to review your spending weekly.
- Keep bills in one folder or app to avoid late fees.

These small systems make life simpler.

They make money easier to manage.

They reduce stress.

They make stability achievable.

Consistency is more important than perfection.

You don't need to do everything perfectly.

Missing a step once does not mean failure.

What matters is showing up again.

Doing it again tomorrow.

And the day after.

Over time, these small habits grow into real stability.

Your money stops slipping through your fingers.

Your stress starts to fade.

Your confidence rises.

The secret is simple: you don’t need complicated strategies or massive changes.

You need small, easy-to-follow habits.

Applied consistently.

When you focus on one habit at a time,

and build simple systems to support it,

you create stability that lasts.

And stability is freedom.

Freedom to plan.

Freedom to grow.

Freedom to live without fear.

PART 4

BUILDING REAL STABILITY

CHAPTER 10
HOW TO STOP LIVING PAYCHECK TO PAYCHECK

Living paycheck to paycheck is exhausting.

It’s a cycle that traps you.

No matter how much you earn, the feeling is the same: you are always behind.

Always stressed.

Always worried.

Always reacting to emergencies instead of planning for your life.

The good news is this: you can break free.

It doesn’t require earning more money.

It doesn’t require luck.

It starts with using what you already have more wisely.

Step One: Plan with what you already have

The first step is clarity.

Take a hard look at your income.

Then look at your bills, your spending, and any debts.

Be honest with yourself.

Don’t judge. Don’t panic.

Just see the truth clearly.

Once you see it, make a simple plan.

Decide which bills must be paid first.

Decide how much you can save, even if it’s small.

Decide where you can make adjustments.

Planning with what you already have gives you control.

It turns money from an enemy into a tool.

Even tiny changes can create breathing room.

Even small adjustments give your mind a sense of relief.

When you plan intentionally, you stop reacting and start acting.

Step Two: Separate needs from wants

This step is simple, but it changes everything.

Ask yourself: what do I really need, and what do I want?

Needs are things you cannot avoid: rent, utilities, groceries.

Wants are things you buy for comfort or fun: coffee, online subscriptions, new gadgets, meals out.

Many people confuse wants with needs.

They buy to feel better temporarily.

They spend to escape stress.

They spend to reward themselves for surviving life’s challenges.

But when wants are treated as needs, money slips away silently.

It disappears before you notice.

And suddenly, the cycle of living paycheck to paycheck continues.

This is not about deprivation.

It is about intention.

Every dollar you spend should serve a purpose: either survival, growth, or meaningful enjoyment.

When you spend intentionally, money becomes a choice instead of a chain.

Step Three: Create breathing room

Even a small buffer makes a huge difference.

A tiny emergency fund—$50, $100, even $200—removes constant fear.

It gives you space to breathe.

It gives your mind a chance to think clearly.

It allows you to plan, instead of reacting.

Breathing room reduces stress, and stress blocks smart decisions.

When fear controls your choices, you spend impulsively.

You avoid planning.

You stay trapped.

But even a little breathing room gives power back to you.

It gives freedom to make better decisions.

It creates a sense of security.

And with that security, you can start building real financial stability.

Step Four: Start small, but start today

Breaking the paycheck-to-paycheck cycle is not about massive changes overnight.

It's about small, consistent steps.

Track your spending.

Set aside a little each week.

Cut one unnecessary expense.

Replace one emotional purchase with a healthier choice.

These small actions compound over time.

One tiny habit becomes a system.

One system becomes stability.

Stability brings freedom.

The truth most people ignore

Most people believe earning more is the answer.

They think a raise or bonus will solve everything.

But without a plan, without clarity, without breathing room, more money disappears just as fast.

The real change comes from control.

Control comes from awareness, intention, and small steps.

When you take control of what you already have,

you stop living paycheck to paycheck.

You stop surviving.

And you start living.

Step Five: Think long-term

Once you have a plan, a clear distinction between needs and wants, and breathing room, start thinking ahead.

Even small savings for emergencies, education, or investment can change your future.

Consistency matters more than speed.

Even $5 a day adds up over time.

Even $20 a week creates freedom.

Remember, freedom is not just about money—it's about choice.

The more control you have over your finances, the more control you have over your life.

The ability to say yes or no, to make decisions without fear, is priceless.

When you apply these steps:

- Planning with what you already have
- Separating needs from wants
- Creating breathing room
- Taking small consistent actions

…you stop living paycheck to paycheck.

And the most powerful part?

Your life changes quietly at first.

You notice less stress.

You notice small victories.

Then one day, you realize:

You are free.

You are in control.

You are finally living.

CHAPTER 11

SAVING WHEN YOU THINK YOU CAN'T

Many people believe they can' t save.

They say, "I don' t make enough," or "There' s never anything left."

But the truth is, saving is not about how much you earn.

It is mental first.

Saving begins in your mind.

It begins with the decision that you can take control.

It begins with believing that even the smallest amount matters.

Because the moment you think saving is impossible,

you stop trying.

And that mindset keeps people trapped.

Tiny amounts that matter

Saving doesn’t have to be huge.

It doesn’t have to be painful.

Even tiny amounts create power over time.

$1 a day.

$5 a week.

$20 a month.

It may seem small now, but it builds momentum.

Over weeks, months, and years, it grows.

The key is consistency, not size.

When you start with small amounts, saving feels possible.

It feels realistic.

It becomes a habit, not a burden.

And habits, even small ones, compound into freedom.

Building safety, not stress

The goal of saving is not to create fear or guilt.

It’s not about depriving yourself.

It’s about creating safety.

A small emergency fund is a buffer against life’s surprises:

A car repair.

A medical bill.

An unexpected expense that used to ruin your month.

With a safety net, you breathe easier.

You make decisions calmly instead of out of panic.

You feel less stress.

You gain confidence.

Saving is not about perfection.

It’ s about starting.

It’ s about building momentum.

It’ s about proving to yourself that you can control your money.

How to start when you feel like you can’ t

1. Decide today: Even if it’ s $1. The moment you decide, you take control.
2. Automate it: Set up a small automatic transfer, so you don’ t have to think about it.
3. Celebrate tiny wins: Each deposit is proof you are making progress.
4. Keep it visible: Watch your savings grow. Seeing even a small number increase is motivating.

The truth is simple: saving is more mental than financial.

Once you overcome the mindset that it’ s impossible,

even the smallest effort creates freedom.

Even tiny savings become a foundation.

Even a little consistency creates peace.

The most powerful part?

When you start saving, no matter how little,

you stop feeling helpless.

You start feeling in control.

You start feeling safe.

And when you feel safe, your life begins to change quietly, steadily, but permanently.

CHAPTER 12

GROWING SLOWLY BUT SAFELY

A lot of people want to get rich fast.

They chase shortcuts, quick wins, or the latest "easy money" idea.

It feels exciting, almost thrilling.

But fast growth comes with hidden risks.

And those risks can wipe out everything you've worked for in an instant.

Real growth is different.

It's slow.

It's steady.

It's careful.

It may feel boring at first, but slow growth builds something strong.

It builds stability that lasts.

Avoiding risky shortcuts

Shortcuts often promise instant success.

They sound smart.

They sound tempting.

But most of the time, they fail.

Think of someone trying to flip a house without experience.

They rush, skip inspections, cut corners.

The project might look like a win at first—but one mistake, one unexpected expense, and it all falls apart.

Safe growth doesn't rely on luck.

It relies on planning, discipline, and patience.

It's about taking steps that feel small today but grow into something big tomorrow.

Like planting a tree—you water it, care for it, and wait.

The tree doesn't sprout overnight, but eventually, it stands tall and strong.

Shortcuts may give a quick burst of growth, but it rarely lasts.

Slow, steady growth creates something permanent.

Why slow growth lasts

Slow growth teaches patience.

It teaches discipline.

It teaches you to handle your money wisely.

Small actions add up:

- Saving a little each week
- Investing carefully
- Tracking your spending
- Avoiding unnecessary debt

These actions may feel insignificant now,

but over months and years, they create real progress.

Fast wins may disappear as quickly as they came.

Slow growth, done consistently, survives life’s storms.

It survives mistakes, emergencies, and surprises.

Imagine someone saving $50 a week.

It may seem tiny, but in a year, that’s $2,600.

Five years later, that’s over $13,000—without touching it.

Small, consistent choices grow into big results.

Thinking long-term

Wealth isn’t about today.

It’ s about tomorrow.

It’ s about next year.

It’ s about ten years from now.

When you think long-term, it changes everything.

You stop chasing instant gratification.

You start making choices that matter.

You begin to see that small, consistent steps create lasting freedom.

Even tiny actions—saving a few dollars, skipping an impulse buy, tracking your money—compound over time.

Consistency and patience beat shortcuts every time.

The reward of slow, safe growth

Slow, safe growth brings more than money.

It brings peace of mind.

It brings confidence.

It gives you control over your life.

It allows you to handle opportunities when they come because you have a strong foundation.

It may feel slow.

It may test your patience.

But in the end, slow growth is the kind that lasts.

It’ s the kind that builds freedom, stability, and real wealth.

Because flashy, fast wins may vanish.

But steady, careful progress sticks.

And that is the real power of growing slowly but safely.

PART 5:

A NEW WAY OF LIVING

CHAPTER 13

MONEY SHOULD SERVE YOU, NOT CONTROL YOU

Most people let money control them.

They live in fear of running out.

They stress over bills, debts, or unexpected expenses.

They let money dictate their choices, their mood, even their self-worth.

But money is a tool.

It is not the boss.

It is not a measure of who you are.

It is meant to serve you—not the other way around.

Changing your relationship with money

Changing the way you think about money is the first step.

Instead of seeing it as a source of stress, see it as a resource.

A way to create opportunities, freedom, and security.

This change begins with awareness.

Track your spending.

Notice where fear or guilt influences your choices.

Ask yourself:

"Am I letting money control me, or am I using it intentionally?"

When you start seeing money as a tool, decisions become easier.

You stop spending out of fear.

You stop hoarding out of anxiety.

You start using your money to move toward goals that matter.

Confidence replaces fear

The real power of this shift is confidence.

Confidence comes from control.

From clarity.

From knowing exactly what you have, where it goes, and how it serves your life.

When fear disappears, confidence takes its place.

You stop worrying about emergencies or “what ifs.”

You make smarter choices.

You feel free to act instead of reacting.

Confidence doesn’t come from having more money.

It comes from understanding the money you already have and using it wisely.

CHAPTER 14

STABILITY IS A LIFESTYLE

Stability is not something you achieve once and forget.

It's not a one-time goal.

It's a way of living.

A series of choices made consistently over time.

Every decision matters—big or small.

The coffee you skip.

The extra shift you take.

The budget you follow.

All of these daily choices build the life you want.

Daily choices

Stability begins with simple, intentional choices.

You don't need to overhaul your life in a day.

You start with what’s in front of you.

- Tracking your spending every day
- Choosing to save a small amount consistently
- Planning meals instead of buying impulsively
- Taking time to review your financial progress

These small choices may feel ordinary, even boring.

But over time, they create a foundation that supports everything else.

Stability grows quietly, almost invisibly, until one day you realize—you’re no longer scrambling.

You’re in control.

Boundaries

Boundaries are a critical part of a stable life.

They protect your money, your time, and your peace.

- Saying no to unnecessary spending
- Setting limits with friends or family who pressure you to overspend
- Protecting your time so you can focus on work, growth, and rest

Boundaries may feel uncomfortable at first.

People might not understand.

But without boundaries, stability is impossible.

They give your life structure, predictability, and safety.

Saying no without guilt

One of the hardest lessons in financial stability is learning to say no.

No to extra expenses.

No to peer pressure.

No to distractions that drain your energy or money.

It’s normal to feel guilty at first.

Society teaches us to say yes.

But saying no is not selfish.

It is self-care.

It is protecting the life you are building.

Every time you say no intentionally, you are saying yes to your future.

Yes to stability.

Yes to freedom.

Yes to peace.

Stability as a lifestyle

When you make stability a lifestyle, it becomes automatic.

It isn't stressful.

It isn't rigid.

It is a natural rhythm of life:

- Thoughtful choices
- Clear boundaries
- Respect for your own limits

And the result?

You live with less fear.

You feel more confident.

You can handle challenges without panic.

You can enjoy life without constantly worrying about money.

Stability isn't a one-time achievement.

It is the sum of daily habits, boundaries, and choices made consistently.

It is a lifestyle—and it is worth every small effort.

Peace as a success measure

Here's the truth most people overlook: success is not just money.

It’s peace.

It’s freedom from fear.

It’s the ability to make choices without being controlled by anxiety about your finances.

When money serves you, life becomes calmer.

Stress fades.

Decisions become clearer.

Opportunities become visible.

You begin to measure success not by how much you earn,

but by how much peace, control, and freedom you feel.

The mindset shift

- Money is a tool, not a master.
- Confidence replaces fear.
- Peace is the ultimate measure of success.

When you adopt this mindset, everything changes.

Spending becomes intentional.

Saving becomes empowering.

Earning becomes purposeful.

Money stops being a source of stress.

It becomes a way to build the life you want.

And when that happens, you are finally in control.

CHAPTER 15

HOW TO STAY FREE

Freedom is not a destination.

It is a daily practice.

It is the result of the choices you make every single day.

Once you break free from fear, debt, and stress, the challenge is staying free.

Old habits have a way of sneaking back in.

Awareness and discipline are the tools that keep you moving forward.

Avoiding old habits

Old habits are the biggest threat to freedom.

Impulse spending, ignoring your budget, emotional buying—they can quietly return if you're not careful.

The key is vigilance.

Notice when you feel tempted to return to old patterns.

Ask yourself:

“Is this choice serving my freedom, or is it pulling me backward?”

When you see the habits coming back, take action immediately.

Even small slips can grow if ignored.

Recognizing them early keeps them from controlling your life again.

Staying aware

Freedom requires awareness.

It’s not enough to set rules and forget about them.

You must stay connected to your finances, your goals, and your priorities.

Track your spending.

Review your progress regularly.

Check in with your emotions around money.

Awareness keeps fear from creeping back.

It prevents stress from taking over.

It ensures that your money works for you, instead of controlling you.

Teaching others what you learned

One of the most powerful ways to stay free is to share your knowledge.

Teaching others—friends, family, even children—reinforces what you have learned.

It reminds you of the lessons you worked hard to master.

It strengthens your habits.

When you help someone else avoid mistakes, you reinforce your own freedom.

You create a network of support, accountability, and encouragement.

Teaching becomes part of your practice.

It keeps you disciplined, aware, and intentional.

The true meaning of freedom

Freedom is not just about money.

It’s about peace.

It’s about control.

It’s about making choices without fear.

It’s about living life intentionally.

To stay free:

- Avoid the habits that trapped you before
- Stay aware of your money and your choices

- Teach others what you have learned

Every day you practice these steps, freedom grows stronger.

Every choice you make reinforces the life you want.

And the longer you stay intentional, the more natural freedom becomes.

Freedom is not something you earn once.

It is something you live, every single day.

CHAPTER 16
YOUR PATH FORWARD

All the lessons you' ve learned so far have one purpose: to give you control.

To help you make choices that build freedom, stability, and peace.

To show you that money is a tool, not a master.

Your path forward is simple—but it requires action.

Nothing changes if you only read these pages.

You must take the principles and put them into practice.

Start with clarity.

Track your money.

Understand what comes in, what goes out, and what truly matters.

Focus on habits.

Small, consistent actions matter more than huge leaps.

Avoid shortcuts. Build slowly.

Prioritize stability over instant gratification.

Protect your freedom.

Stay aware. Avoid old habits.

Set boundaries.

Say no when necessary, without guilt.

And most importantly, share what you’ve learned.

Teach someone else.

Accountability strengthens your own progress.

Helping others creates a ripple effect of freedom.

CHAPTER 17

THE LIFE YOU DESERVE

You deserve a life where money does not control you.

A life where fear is replaced with confidence.

A life where choices are made intentionally, not out of stress or panic.

The life you deserve is not built overnight.

It is built one decision at a time.

One habit at a time.

One small action repeated consistently.

Imagine waking up without fear of bills.

Imagine making choices without stress or guilt.

Imagine having the freedom to pursue opportunities because you have a foundation that supports you.

This is possible.

It is within your reach.

And it starts with the first step:

Deciding to take control today.

Final Thoughts - Freedom is Your Choice

Freedom is not about money alone.

It is about peace.

It is about control.

It is about living intentionally.

The strategies in this book—clarity, habits, slow growth, awareness—are not magic.

They are practical.

They are proven.

They work when you apply them consistently.

The choice is yours:

Keep living paycheck to paycheck, controlled by fear and habits you cannot sustain…

Or take the lessons in this book, apply them, and create a life where money serves you, not the other way around.

Freedom is not a dream.

It is a decision.

A lifestyle.

A series of choices you make every day.

Start today. Take control.

Your future self will thank you.

Conclusion - You Are in Control

You’ve learned a lot in this book.

You’ve discovered that money doesn’t have to control you.

You’ve learned that clarity, habits, patience, and awareness create freedom.

You’ve seen that slow, steady growth lasts longer than risky shortcuts.

But knowledge alone is not enough.

The real power comes when you take action.

When you make one choice today that moves you closer to stability.

When you start one small habit that grows into lasting peace.

You are capable of more than you realize.

You have the ability to change your relationship with money.

To break free from stress.

To live intentionally.

Remember:

- Small steps matter.
- Consistency beats perfection.
- Freedom is built one choice at a time.

There will be challenges.

Old habits may try to return.

Fear and doubt may appear.

That’s normal.

Every person who achieves freedom faces these moments.

The difference is persistence.

The difference is deciding that your future is more important than a temporary comfort.

Believe in yourself.

Celebrate your small wins.

Keep moving forward, even if progress feels slow.

You are in control.

Your life is in your hands.

Money can serve you, your goals, and your dreams.

Take what you’ve learned.

Apply it.

And step into the life you deserve—one of freedom, stability, and peace.

You can do this.

Your future is waiting.

Action Plan – Your Roadmap to Financial Freedom

Use this guide to take control of your money, build stability, and create lasting freedom. Each step is small but powerful. Start today.

Step 1 – Get Clear

- Track every dollar coming in and going out.
- Know exactly where your money is going.
- Focus on awareness, not perfection.

Step 2 – Stop Living Paycheck to Paycheck

- Separate needs from wants.
- Create breathing room with a small buffer or emergency fund.
- Plan your spending intentionally.

Step 3 – Build Small, Powerful Habits

- Start with one habit at a time.
- Automate savings, track spending, or plan meals.
- Be consistent; small actions compound over time.

Step 4 – Avoid Shortcuts, Grow Safely

- Say no to risky "get rich quick" schemes.
- Focus on slow, steady growth.
- Think long-term—small, repeated steps create lasting results.

Step 5 – Change Your Money Mindset

- See money as a tool, not a master.
- Replace fear with confidence.
- Measure success by peace, not just earnings.

Step 6 – Protect Your Freedom

- Avoid old habits that drain your money.
- Set boundaries for spending, time, and energy.
- Say no without guilt—it's protecting your future.

Step 7 – Stay Aware Every Day

- Track your progress regularly.
- Notice emotional spending or impulses.
- Adjust your habits before small slips become big problems.

Step 8 – Teach and Share

- Share what you learn with family or friends.
- Teaching others reinforces your habits.
- Create accountability and support networks.

Step 9 - Celebrate Wins and Keep Going

- Acknowledge small victories—they matter.
- Keep building momentum, even if progress feels slow.
- Freedom is a lifestyle, not a one-time achievement.

Remember:

You don’t need more money to start.

You need clarity, intention, and consistent action.

Every small step you take today creates stability, peace, and freedom for tomorrow.

Take control. Start now.

Your life, your freedom, and your future are waiting.

www.ingramcontent.com/pod-product-compliance
Lightning Source LLC
LaVergne TN
LVHW022021200926
848481LV00007B/2478
* 9 7 9 8 3 4 8 4 5 8 0 1 0 *